THE USBORNE
STORY OF
MUSIC

Eileen O'Brien

Designed by Rebecca Halverson
Additional designs by Lucy Parris

Illustrated by David Cuzik
Cover photography by Howard Allman

Edited by Emma Danes and Caroline Hooper
Series editor: Jane Chisholm
Music consultant: Ruth Thackeray

CONTENTS

Music in ancient times

The story of music goes back to prehistoric times. Even before people started making instruments, they made sounds, probably by singing, clapping or hitting things. Originally these sounds may have been used as signals, but people soon began to organize them into musical patterns.

The type of flute in this picture was very popular in Egypt.

This cave painting shows people clapping. It is more than 10,000 years old.

Most of the evidence for musical activity in ancient times comes from pictures, but some very early instruments have also been found.

This whistle was made in France about 15,000 years ago.

Egyptian music

In ancient Egypt, over 4,000 years ago, music played a large part in everyday life. Dancers and flute players accompanied work such as planting crops. Other musicians, usually women, entertained kings and noblemen at court. Some people studied music in special academies.

Music and religion

Music was very important in Egyptian religious ceremonies. Gods and goddesses were often shown in paintings playing instruments.

A carving of the Egyptian goddess Isis holding a rattle called a sistrum

Greek music

The word 'music' comes from an old Greek word, *mousike*, after the nine Greek muses, who were goddesses of art and science. Around 2,500 years ago, music was so important that people thought it was the invention of the gods. They told stories about gods and the magic powers of the music they made. Two instruments used by the Greeks were a wind instrument called an *aulos* and a stringed instrument called a *kithara*.

Aulos

Kithara

Greek festivals

Ceremonies involving music and dancing were held in praise of the Greek god of plays and wine, Dionysus. These included a singing competition held each year in Athens. People wore costumes and there was dancing as well.

Greek dancers and musicians at a festival in praise of Dionysus

Roman music

In Rome, over 2,000 years ago, concerts were held in wealthy people's villas and in public. Some parts of plays were also set to music.

This picture shows a Roman pipe player and actors preparing to go on stage.

The Roman actors in the picture below are performing a play. They are accompanied by musicians.

Musicians were usually slaves, although they were often well paid for giving concerts. Some rich people learned to play instruments, but they didn't play in public, as people thought it was undignified.

Jugglers and acrobats often performed in the Roman city streets. Musicians sometimes played drums, pipes and tambourines alongside them.

This is a Roman street musician.

Roman musicians and dancers sometimes performed in this area.

The audience sat in rows of stone seats.

This is the stage where the actors performed.

Medieval music

The Christian religion was very important in daily life in Europe during the Middle Ages. Music played a large part in church ceremonies and services.

Most religious music involved singing a simple melody, or tune. This was called plainsong, or plainchant. One type of plainsong is called Gregorian chant. The songs were usually sung by a choir, without instruments, but a small organ was sometimes used.

Hildegard of Bingen with a monk

A group of monks singing at a church service.

Among the first composers whose name we know is a German nun called Hildegard of Bingen (1098-1179). She wrote lots of religious poems which she set to simple melodies.

A new style

From the end of the 9th century, composers began to write two or more lines of melody which were sung at the same time. This style is known as polyphony. The French composer Léonin (who lived around 1163-1201) was among the first known composers to write two lines to be sung together. Around 1200, a composer called Pérotin began to write three or four.

Writing music down

The way we write down music today began to develop in the Middle Ages. At first, marks were placed over the words to show singers roughly what to sing.

This picture shows how music was first written down.

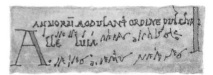

Soon these marks were placed on lines. Each line, and space between the lines, stood for a different note, so the singer knew exactly which notes to sing.

Monks wrote down plainsong melodies in books, which were often beautifully decorated. They were kept in monasteries and churches throughout Europe.

On the right is part of a 13th-century song book.

Minstrels

Music was also used for entertainment. From around the 10th century, men and women called minstrels went from place to place singing songs, playing instruments, juggling and performing acrobatics.

Minstrels often dressed up in masks and costumes.

This scene shows a group of French minstrels, known as jongleurs.

A snake-shaped horn

These men are playing wind instruments called shawms.

A lute

A horn

This man is playing a harp.

A fiddle

The jongleurs are on their way to a town to perform.

This man is playing a stringed instrument called a hurdy gurdy.

Some noblemen became famous poets and composers. They were known as *troubadours* or *trouvères* in France and *Minnesinger* in Germany. They performed for kings and wealthy people, and they usually sang simple love songs.

These troubadours are playing a rebec and a lute.

The 'new art'

From the beginning of the 14th century, composers such as Guillaume de Machaut (around 1300 -1377) began to write music with more complicated rhythms and adventurous melodies. This new musical style became known as *ars nova* which means 'new art'.

Renaissance music

In Europe, during the 15th and 16th centuries, there was a great interest in art, music and learning. This time became known as the Renaissance, which means 'rebirth'.

These people are attending a university lecture.

A flute

A bass viol

This man is playing a treble viol.

This man is playing a lute.

In this picture, musicians are playing for dancers at court.

Music for entertainment

During the Renaissance, many composers began to work at the courts of wealthy noblemen, kings and princes.

They wrote music to entertain people, such as dance music for courtiers, as well as for church services.

The Duke of Burgundy in France employed some of the best composers and musicians in Europe. They included Guillaume Dufay (who lived around 1398-1474) and Gilles Binchois (around 1400-1460).

Music printing

Printing was invented in Germany around 1450. The first music book was printed in Italy by Ottaviano de Petrucci in 1501.

This is a 16th-century printing press.

Before this, music was copied out by hand, which took a long time and was very expensive. Printing meant that music books could be made quickly and cheaply. Soon music was being printed throughout Europe.

Lots of composers had their music printed during the Renaissance, including Josquin des Près (around 1440-1521).

Guillaume Dufay   *Gilles Binchois*

Both these composers wrote French songs called *chansons*.

Music for amateurs

Before the Renaissance, instruments were usually played by professional musicians. Now rich people began to learn instruments such as the lute just for pleasure.

This woman is playing a lute.

The dancers could only take small steps in their stiff and heavy clothing.

Madrigals

During the Renaissance, songs called madrigals became very popular. They were often about love and were sung in small groups, without any musical instruments.

Madrigals were first written in Italy but they soon spread throughout Europe. Andrea Gabrieli (1533-1585), who worked in Italy, wrote lots of famous madrigals.

These people are singing a madrigal.

Instrumental music

Before the 16th century, instruments were mainly used to accompany singers. From around 1500 however, people started to compose music specially for instruments. Instrumental music was often used with dancing. You can see some instruments used below.

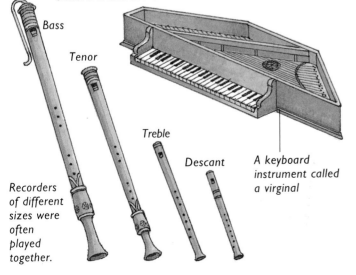

Bass

Tenor

Treble

Descant

A keyboard instrument called a virginal

Recorders of different sizes were often played together.

Church music

Some composers, such as the Italian Giovanni Palestrina (around 1525-1594), still wrote mostly church music. New types of church music also began to develop. Thomas Tallis (around 1505-1585) started to write music for the whole congregation to sing, not just the choir.

Baroque music

Baroque is the name given to European music from about 1600 to 1750. During this time, instrumental music became more important, and lots of new types of music were written. One of the most important changes was the invention of opera (see pages 16-17).

Lots of organ music was written during the Baroque period.

Instruments such as the flute were improved so that more notes could be played on them. Some people wrote books on how to play instruments.

Unlike modern metal flutes, Baroque flutes were made of wood.

The concerto grosso

A *concerto grosso* is a piece of music for a small group of solo instruments and an orchestra. Some famous concertos include *The Four Seasons* (written around 1725) by Antonio Vivaldi (1678-1741), and the six Brandenburg concertos (written in 1721) by the German composer Johann Sebastian Bach (1685-1750).

A small Baroque orchestra

Oratorios

An *oratorio* is a religious story, performed by a choir, an orchestra and solo singers. Unlike opera, the singers don't act out the parts. *Messiah*, by George Frideric Handel (1685-1759), is a famous oratorio.

Violin makers

The violin was very popular during the Baroque period, especially in Italy. Some violin makers, such as Antonio Stradivari (1644-1737) who worked in Cremona in Italy, became very famous. The violins made in his workshop are especially valuable today.

A Stradivarius violin

Writing music down

Composers began to write marks on their music to tell players whether to play loudly or softly. They mainly used Italian words. This system is still used today.

The word 'piano' is Italian for quiet. It tells the player to play quietly.

Public concerts

Until the 17th century, most musicians were employed by wealthy people, to play music in their own homes. They were also employed by the Church. Public concerts, where the audience paid to see a performance, began in the Baroque period. This meant that composers no longer had to rely entirely on the Church or the court for their livelihood. Handel made his living mostly from staging his operas and oratorios.

Suites

Some composers began to write several dances to be played one after the other. These sets were known as suites. The French composer Jean-Philippe Rameau (1683-1764) wrote lots of suites for keyboard instruments such as the harpsichord.

A Baroque harpsichord

A public performance of one of Handel's oratorios in London, England

Classical music

The word 'classical' is often used to describe all music that isn't pop, folk or jazz. But it really means music from the late 18th to the early 19th centuries. During this time, public concerts became very popular. A lot of Baroque music, such as the concerto and sonata, developed into the forms we know today.

These 18th-century musicians are playing a string quartet (music for two violins, viola and cello).

Haydn

A performance of one of Haydn's operas at Eszterháza, in Hungary. Haydn is seated at the harpsichord.

For most of his life, the Austrian composer Joseph Haydn (1732-1809) worked for the Esterházy family in Hungary. He was in charge of all of the palace musicians, and had to provide music for two concerts a week.

Mozart

At the age of four, Wolfgang Amadeus Mozart (1756-1791) could already play difficult pieces on the harpsichord and organ. He spent his life composing, teaching and conducting his works throughout Europe.

As a child, Mozart gave many concerts in European cities.

Beethoven

Ludwig van Beethoven (1770-1827) developed a way of writing music which influenced many composers of the Romantic period (see pages 14-15). At the time, some people thought that his music was very complicated.

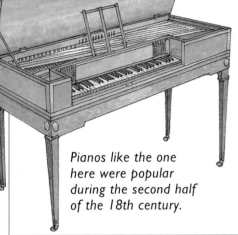

Pianos

The piano was invented around 1700 in Italy by Bartolomeo Cristofori. The proper name for a piano is *pianoforte*, which is Italian for soft-loud. Unlike the harpsichord, you can play both loud (*forte*) and soft (*piano*) on a piano.

Pianos like the one here were popular during the second half of the 18th century.

The sonata

Cover of a piano sonata by Mozart

During the Baroque period, the term sonata was used to describe many different types of instrumental compositions. The Classical sonata developed from this into a piece for one or two instruments. Most sonatas are for piano alone, or for another instrument accompanied by a piano. Sonatas are usually in three or four sections, called movements.

The concerto

The Classical concerto developed from the Baroque concerto (see page 8). It is a piece for orchestra with one or more soloists. The music played by the soloist is often more difficult and exciting than that played by the orchestra.

A performance of a Classical flute concerto

The symphony

Beethoven watching the conductor at a performance of one of his symphonies.

The word symphony means 'sounding together'. The symphony developed from the Baroque *sinfonia*, a piece played at the start of an Italian opera. A Classical symphony is a piece for orchestra and it usually has four movements.

The orchestra

The word 'orchestra' comes from a Greek word meaning 'dancing place'. In ancient times, it was the place where singers and dancers performed. Later, it was used to describe a part of the stage where musicians sat. By the 1700s, the word meant the players themselves. Orchestras are made up of four groups of instruments: strings, woodwind, brass and percussion.

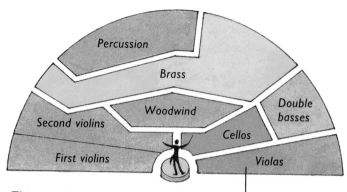

This is a plan of the orchestra in the picture below.

The cellos sometimes sit here.

The conductor

A conductor leads an orchestra by waving his hands, or a stick called a baton. The conductor decides how fast or slow the music should be, and how loud or soft each part should be played.

During the 17th and 18th centuries, orchestras almost always included a keyboard instrument, such as a harpsichord or organ. The orchestra was conducted by the person playing the keyboard instrument, or by the leading violinist, from their place in the orchestra.

Percussion

Percussion can mean any instrument, or object, that makes a sound when you hit it, scrape it or shake it. Until around 1850, the most common percussion instrument was a type of drum called a kettledrum, or timpanum. Composers soon began to use instruments such as bells and xylophones as well. In 20th-century music, the percussion section is often very large.

Kettledrum

Cymbals

Tambourine

Triangle

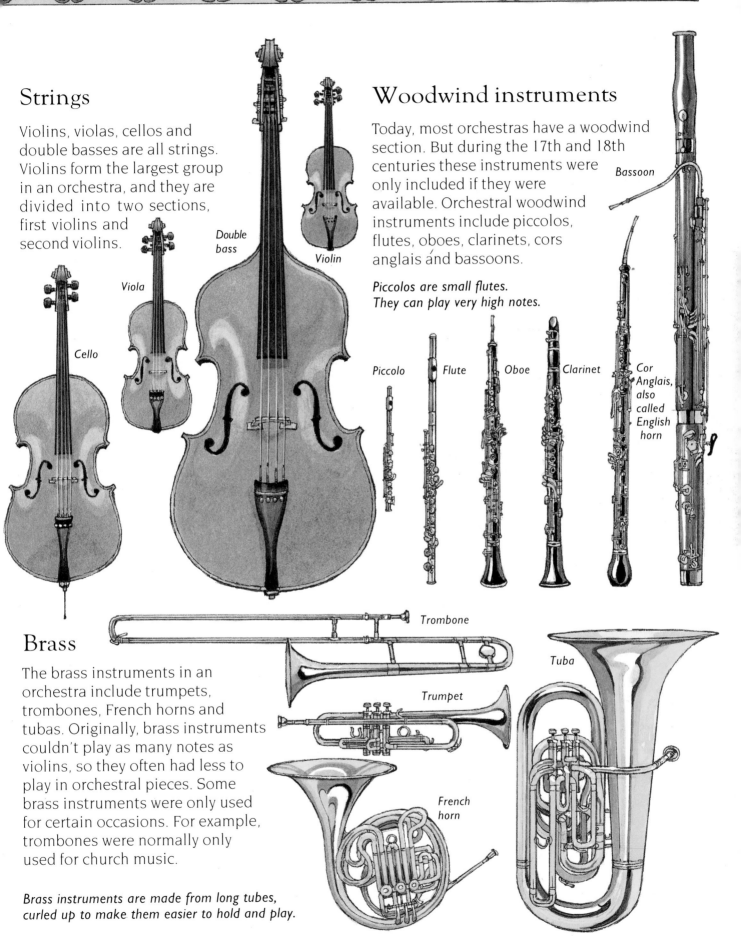

Strings

Violins, violas, cellos and double basses are all strings. Violins form the largest group in an orchestra, and they are divided into two sections, first violins and second violins.

Cello

Viola

Double bass

Violin

Woodwind instruments

Today, most orchestras have a woodwind section. But during the 17th and 18th centuries these instruments were only included if they were available. Orchestral woodwind instruments include piccolos, flutes, oboes, clarinets, cors anglais and bassoons.

Piccolos are small flutes. They can play very high notes.

Bassoon

Piccolo *Flute* *Oboe* *Clarinet* *Cor Anglais, also called English horn*

Brass

The brass instruments in an orchestra include trumpets, trombones, French horns and tubas. Originally, brass instruments couldn't play as many notes as violins, so they often had less to play in orchestral pieces. Some brass instruments were only used for certain occasions. For example, trombones were normally only used for church music.

Brass instruments are made from long tubes, curled up to make them easier to hold and play.

Trombone

Tuba

Trumpet

French horn

Romantic music

The 19th century is often referred to as the Romantic period. Some composers of Romantic music intended particular feelings to be associated with it. Their music was often inspired by poems, paintings, nature and stories. Many 19th-century musicians became very famous. Some soloists had lots of fans, and were treated like pop stars today.

Balls, like the one in the picture, were often held in Vienna during this period. The waltz was the most popular dance.

The Polish pianist Paderewski (1860-1941) was often mobbed by audiences during his concerts.

The waltz

During the Romantic period, a dance known as the waltz became very fashionable in Vienna, Austria. Composers such as Johann Strauss (1825-1899) wrote many famous waltzes, including *The Blue Danube*. The waltz was often performed in large coffee houses and ballrooms.

Eastern Europe

Many 19th century composers, especially in eastern Europe, became very interested in the folk music and traditions of their countries. Around the middle of the century, a group of Russian composers began to write music based on the folk songs and dances of Russia. They became known as the 'Mighty handful'.

These dancers are performing a Russian folk dance.

Many people thought that the waltz was unhealthy, as some couples whirled around the room very quickly.

Symphonic poems

Franz Liszt

Composers sometimes wrote instrumental music which told a story. This type of music was known as a symphonic poem. There were no words, but if you knew the story you could hear it in the music itself. The Hungarian composer Franz Liszt (1811-1886) wrote many famous symphonic poems, including *Hamlet* (written in 1858), which is based on a play by William Shakespeare.

Schubert's songs

People often invited friends to their homes to play music for each other. A composer called Franz Schubert (1797-1828) arranged musical evenings for his friends and family. The songs that he wrote, called *Lieder*, were very popular.

Schubert himself often accompanied a singer on the piano.

The symphony

Many composers continued to write symphonies and concertos, but they were usually on a much larger scale than before. Romantic symphonies like those of Gustav Mahler (1860-1911) are longer than most Classical symphonies. Some of them, such as his 8th Symphony, were written for very large orchestras.

Mahler based some of his symphonies on a collection of poetry.

Opera

An opera is like a play where some or all of the words are sung. The first operas were written in the 1590s, in Italy, by a group of poets and composers called the *Camerata*.

Early opera

One of the most famous early operas is *Orfeo*, by Claudio Monteverdi (1567-1643), first performed in Italy in 1607.

On the right is a scene from a 17th-century opera. Complicated machinery was needed for the moving clouds.

Some of the earliest French operas were written by Jean-Baptiste Lully (1632-1687) for the court of King Louis XIV.

Louis XIV in ballet costume

They usually included ballet dancing, because the King, who was a good dancer, liked to take part in them. Spectacular costumes and scenery were used in most of Lully's operas.

Opera seria

At first, operas were very serious. The stories were taken from ancient history, or were about gods and goddesses. In the 1700s, this type of opera was known as *opera seria*, which means 'serious opera'. George Frideric Handel (1685-1759) was a famous *opera seria* composer.

Comic opera

Composers soon began to write operas in a lighter, comic style. In Italy, this new type of opera was known as *opera buffa*. In Germany, it was called *Singspiel*. These operas often included spoken words.

Backstage preparations for an 18th-century performance of Mozart's Singspiel, 'The Magic Flute'

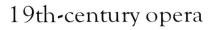

19th-century opera

During the 19th century, some very famous operas were written, especially by Italian composers such as Giuseppe Verdi (1813-1901) and Giacomo Puccini (1858-1924).

A scene from Puccini's opera 'Turandot'

Around 1830, a new type of opera, called 'grand opera', began to develop. The stories were often based on legends. Grand operas, such as *Guillaume Tell* (1829) by Gioachino Rossini (1792-1868), often included crowd scenes, involving lots of singers.

Operetta

Another style of opera that became popular in the 1800s was operetta. It developed from 18th-century French comic opera, known as *opéra comique*. Operettas were light-hearted, with some words spoken as well as sung. They were shorter than other operas and included dances.

From the front cover of the operetta 'Die Fledermaus' by Johann Strauss II (1825-1899)

20th-century opera

In the early 1900s, composers such as Igor Stravinsky (1882-1971) began to write operas using the forms and techniques of Baroque and Classical composers. In 1922, he wrote *Mavra* in this style. Other composers have experimented with new ways of writing and performing operas. For example, Luigi Nono (1924-1990) used recorded sounds in his opera *Intolleranza*.

This is a scene from 'The Mask of Orpheus', by the English composer Harrison Birtwistle (born 1934).

Music and dance

Most dances are accompanied by some sort of music. The first dances were probably part of religious ceremonies. But, by the time of the ancient Greeks and Romans, people danced at festivals and celebrations, and dances were included in plays.

The ancient Greeks associated dance with religion and drama.

The Middle Ages

Dancing was very popular in Europe during the Middle Ages. We know this from pictures and books of the time. People danced to lots of different instruments including drums, lutes, bagpipes and trumpets. Some dances were also accompanied by singers.

The people in the picture below are performing a dance called a branle. They are accompanied by a man playing bagpipes.

Dancing at court

In the Renaissance and Baroque periods (pages 6-9), lots of dances were performed at royal courts. Dance teachers, or dancing masters, were employed not only to teach people how to dance, but also how to move around gracefully.

During the Baroque period, a dance called a minuet was often performed at court.

Folk dancing

Dancing has always been a part of everyday life. Every country has its own tradition of folk music and dancing. People dance for entertainment, at celebrations, and sometimes while they are working. Folk dances have changed gradually over the years, as they have been passed on to different generations, and as people went to different parts of the world. Like music, folk dances are often influenced by other dance styles.

A drum dance from Korea

Ballet

Ballet is a type of dance which tells a story, often with amazing costumes and scenery. Ballet began in European courts at the end of the 16th century. It was especially popular in Russia during the 19th century. Composers such as Pyotr Il'yich Tchaikovsky (1840-1893) wrote the music for some very famous ballets, including *Swan Lake* (1877) and *The Sleeping Beauty* (1890).

Costumes like the ones on the left were worn by dancers in the 17th century at the court of Louis XIV in France.

A scene from 'The Sleeping Beauty' by Tchaikovsky

Dancing for fun

People have always danced for fun. Most people learn to dance by watching or copying other people. Styles of dancing change constantly, as fashion and music change. During the 1960s, a dance style called the twist became popular. People invented their own steps, using simple, repetitive movements.

The twist became very popular with the hit song 'Let's Twist Again', made famous by Chubby Checker (born 1941).

Blues

Blues was developed in the early 20th century by African-American people in the southern states of the USA. The ancestors of most African-Americans were slaves. They were brought from Africa, to work in the USA, between the 17th and the early 19th centuries.

Violin

Bones

Banjo

These slaves from the early 19th century are dancing and playing instruments.

Blues has its roots in some of the music of these slaves, such as religious music and songs they sang while they worked. Blues songs often tell stories about the hard lives that many African-American people led.

Minstrel shows

Many early blues musicians, such as W.C. Handy (1873-1958), took part in shows called minstrel shows. Groups of minstrels performed slaves' songs and dances all over the USA. They were very popular throughout the country.

A minstrel group from the 1840s

Blues styles

In the early 20th century, various types of blues began to develop. In the 1930s, a style called country blues became popular. The songs often described the hardship of everyday life in the country.

Country blues musicians often made their own instruments, like those on the right.

This man is playing a washboard.

A homemade guitar, played by sliding a bottle along a single string

This singer is humming through paper stretched over a comb.

A different style, known as city blues, was played in cities such as Chicago. Many musicians played loud instruments, such as the saxophone or trumpet, which were easy to hear in noisy clubs. Bands were often larger than country blues bands.

Trumpet

Saxophone

Blues stars

During the 1950s, blues music became very popular among young people in the USA and Europe. Performers such as B.B. King, Son House and John Lee Hooker often played for huge audiences.

B.B. King

Jazz

Like blues, jazz first appeared around the beginning of the 20th century. It was played in and around New Orleans, by African-American people. Jazz grew out of many different types of music that were popular in the 19th century, including music played by brass bands and slaves.

A brass band from New Orleans at the beginning of the 20th century

Jazz was first played by bands in dance halls and bars, as well as for social occasions. It soon spread to other parts of the USA and Europe.

An early jazz band

Few of the early jazz players could read music, so lots of it was made up, or improvised, as they went along. Jazz is still sometimes improvised today.

Swing bands

In the 1920s and 30s, large jazz bands, which often had a violin section, were very popular. They were known as swing bands, and they made lots of records which were played on the radio and in films.

These record labels are from records of famous swing bands.

Modern jazz

From the 1940s, jazz performances began to include more and more solo parts. Solos played by musicians, such as the trumpeter Dizzie Gillespie, were often very difficult, with lots of complicated rhythms.

Dizzie Gillespie

Jazz influence

Jazz has had a great influence on both popular and classical music. Many composers, such as Aaron Copland (born 1900) and Claude Debussy (1862-1918), have used elements of jazz in their music.

Trombone · Trumpet · Saxophone · Clarinet · Drums · Violin · Double bass

Music in the 20th century

The music of the 20th century includes a great variety of styles. Some pieces, such as *The Cave* by Steve Reich (born 1936), make use of the latest technology. As well as using traditional instruments and singers, the music is accompanied by words and pictures displayed on five large screens. Other composers have continued to use older forms, such as symphonies and concertos.

A performance of 'The Cave' by Steve Reich

Riot at the ballet

In 1913, a ballet called *The Rite of Spring*, by Igor Stravinsky (1882-1971) was first performed in Paris. The music was unlike anything the audience had heard before.

Some people were so upset by what they heard and saw that a riot began. Those who wanted to enjoy it struggled with those who wanted it stopped.

Some original costume designs for 'The Rite of Spring'

Electronic music

After tape recorders were invented in the 1940s, many composers began to use recorded sounds in their pieces. Some performances involve taped sounds together with instruments or voices.

Karlheinz Stockhausen (born 1928) uses electronic sounds in his music.

Aleatory music

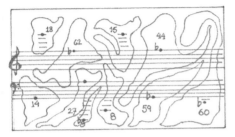

Part of 'Concert for piano and orchestra' by the composer John Cage (born 1912). The music is written as different shapes around a main note.

One new type of music is called aleatory music. The performer decides how to play the piece, choosing which notes to play and how long to hold them. The music is written as shapes, lines or patterns.

Computers

Later in the 20th century, composers began to use computers to write and record music. Special computer programs have been developed to help compose the music itself, following the composer's instructions. The piece can then be played back through a synthesizer. A composer can hear his or her music before it is performed. Computers also make it easier to write music down.

In this picture, a clarinet is connected to a computer. The music is stored in the computer's memory.

New sounds

Some composers have experimented with new sounds in their music. In his travels around France, a composer called Olivier Messiaen (1908-1992) listened to different types of birdsongs. In some of his music, such as *Catalogue d'oiseaux* for piano, he used sounds that resemble birds singing. Other composers have used unusual percussion instruments. For example, Edgar Varèse (1883-1965) wrote a piece called *Ionisation* for percussion instruments, which included chains, anvils and sirens.

The percussion instruments used in this picture include a siren, a typewriter and bottles.

Some unusual instruments used in 20th century music

A radio

A plunger

A scrubbing brush

Chains

Popular music

A lighter kind of music, known as popular music, has always existed alongside classical music. Popular music is usually considered to be music that entertains lots of people. It can include folk music, as well as blues, jazz and different kinds of rock and pop.

Music halls

In the 19th century, singers and musicians often performed in large halls, known as music halls. Songs sung in music halls were rather like the hits of today, and they appealed to a wide audience.

Music Hall star Harry Lauder

Recording

Recording equipment was invented in 1877. In the early 1900s, performers such as Cole Porter (1891-1964) made records of their music, which people played on gramophones, or listened to on the radio. This meant that popular music could be heard by a bigger audience.

Cole Porter

Rock and roll

Teenagers dancing to music on a juke box in the 1950s

During the 1950s, a style of music called rock and roll became very popular among young people. At first, the most successful rock and roll stars, such as Elvis Presley, came from America. By the 1960s, rock and roll had spread to Europe. A British band called The Beatles became the first group outside America to become world famous.

Musicals

A musical is a play which includes songs and dances. It developed in the USA in the early 20th century from operetta (see page 17) and music hall. Early musicals, such as *Oklahoma* by Richard Rogers and Oscar Hammerstein II, were light-hearted, and songs were usually catchy or sentimental. More recently, musicals like *Cats* by Andrew Lloyd Webber, have been influenced by rock.

A scene from the musical 'Oliver'

Rock music

Rock music ranges from quiet ballads to songs that include complicated electric guitar solos. It first developed during the 1960s, when rock concerts and festivals, starring bands such as The Rolling Stones, attracted huge crowds. Other singers, such as Bob Dylan, used a mixture of folk and rock in their songs.

Mick Jagger from The Rolling Stones performing at an open-air concert in the early 70s

Popular music in recent times

Some of the most famous pop stars of the twentieth century included Michael Jackson, Madonna, and Prince. Their music appealed to a wide audience. One of the biggest rock bands of the 1980s was U2. Other 80s styles included rap, reggae, heavy metal and punk.

Today, many bands mix different styles. The music of Nirvana, for example, uses elements of punk, heavy metal and pop. This style is known as 'grunge'. Hip-hop is also a very popular music style in recent times.

Kurt Cobain (1967-1994), the lead singer for Nirvana

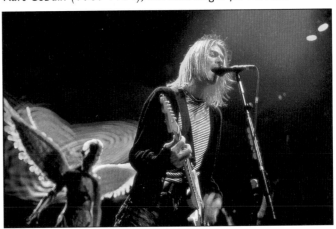

A heavy metal artist

A reggae artist

A punk artist

A rap artist

Music in the Middle East

The Middle East is the area just east of Europe. It is made up mainly of Arabic-speaking countries which follow the Muslim religion, known as Islam.

Some music that was first played at courts over 1,200 years ago is still popular today. It usually involves singing and a few instruments.

Middle Eastern music is based on patterns of notes, called modes. Musicians make up, or improvise, the music as they play, based on these modes.

Religion

Music is not used very much in Islam, the main religion in the Middle East, except for chanting prayers.

This singer is calling people to prayer from the tower of a muslim place of worship.

A spike fiddle   *A singer*   *A duff*   *A naqqāra*

A group of Arab musicians. Their instruments include a fiddle, which is played resting on the ground, and two types of drums.

Music in everyday life

Farmers and shepherds often sing while they work, and dancing is popular at festivals and celebrations, such as weddings and births. Dances are often accompanied by singing, clapping or instruments. A dance called the *Al-Ardha* is one of the most popular dances. Performers play drums as they dance.

North African dancers accompanied by duff players

Influence in Europe

Middle Eastern music has had a strong influence on music in Europe. Between the 8th and the 15th centuries, armies from North Africa invaded Spain. Middle Eastern influence can be seen in some Spanish music and in modern Spanish flamenco dances. In the early Middle Ages, European armies went to the Middle East and brought back some of the instruments they heard. Two of these were stringed instruments called the *'ūd* and *rabāb*. In Europe, they became known as the lute and rebec.

'Ūd (lute)

Rabāb (rebec)

Music in Africa

Africa is the second largest continent in the world. It is made up of many different races of people, each with its own musical tradition.

These dancers are from Mozambique.

Xylophone

This drum is played with a stick.

A drum made from a painted oil drum

They are performing a dance called the Inzumba step dance.

In many parts of Africa, music is played at festivals and other celebrations. People often sing or play as they work. Music is also used in religious ceremonies. Some people believe that music is a link with the spirit world.

African songs often involve a solo singer, who acts as a leader, and a chorus.

African drums

African music is often accompanied by drums. Many drums are made from hollowed logs and animal skins. People play them with sticks or their hands.

This drum comes from Ghana.

This drum from Zambia is made from a log with a slit in it.

Drums are often played in large groups, with each of the drummers playing a different rhythm. These rhythms combine to make a very complicated sound.

Some drummers can imitate speech by changing the tightness of the skin on a special 'talking' drum. As the skin gets tighter, the sound gets higher.

This man is playing a Nigerian talking drum.

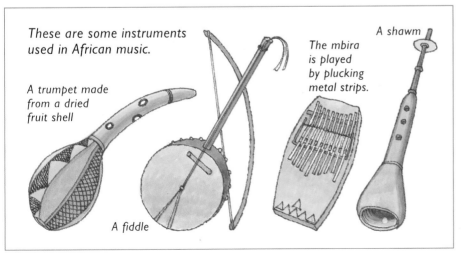

These are some instruments used in African music.

A trumpet made from a dried fruit shell

A fiddle

The mbira is played by plucking metal strips.

A shawm

Music in the Far East

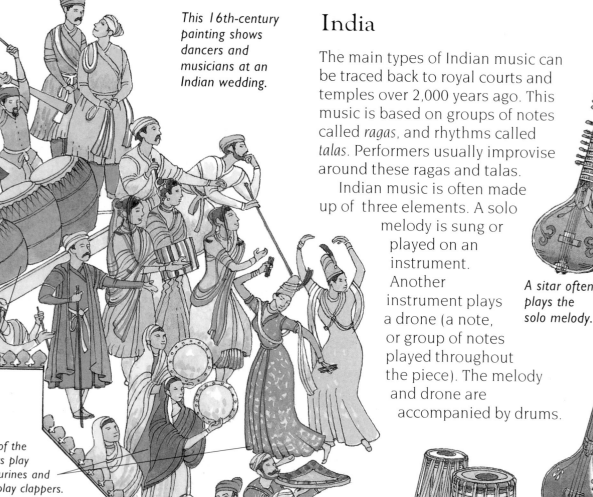

Horns

This 16th-century painting shows dancers and musicians at an Indian wedding.

Drums

Some of the dancers play tambourines and some play clappers.

These people take offerings of spices to the Emperor who is going to be married.

India

The main types of Indian music can be traced back to royal courts and temples over 2,000 years ago. This music is based on groups of notes called *ragas*, and rhythms called *talas*. Performers usually improvise around these ragas and talas.

Indian music is often made up of three elements. A solo melody is sung or played on an instrument. Another instrument plays a drone (a note, or group of notes played throughout the piece). The melody and drone are accompanied by drums.

A sitar often plays the solo melody.

Tablā

A tambūrā often plays the drone.

Japan

In Japan, music accompanies a type of play called kabuki. These plays involve dancing, and the performers often wear beautiful costumes. All the actors are men, even those who play women's characters. The actors themselves do not sing, but singers sometimes form part of the orchestra. Singers are usually accompanied by melody instruments called shamisens.

One of the oldest Japanese instruments is a stringed instrument called a koto. The player presses the strings with one hand, and plucks them with the other.

The koto has 13 strings stretched over pieces of wood.

China

Beijing opera is a type of Chinese opera that developed in the late 18th century from older types of Chinese drama. The opera includes dancing and acrobatics as well as singing. Here are some instruments used in the orchestra.

This is a scene from a Beijing opera.

A plucked stringed instrument called a p'i p'a

A Chinese drum

A Chinese mouth organ called a sheng

Indonesia

Indonesian orchestras, called gamelans, are made up mainly of percussion instruments (ones you hit), such as gongs and drums. Gamelans are played at parties and religious festivals. They are also used in Indonesian puppet shows.

This gamelan is from Bali in Indonesia.

Gongs

Metallophones are instruments like xylophones but with metal rather than wooden bars.

This is an Indonesian puppet.

Barrel drum

Music to listen to

On these two pages, there are some suggestions for music to listen to. Most of the recordings can be found in music stores and libraries. When a specific recording has been recommended, the record label is shown in brackets. If you can't find some of the recordings, try listening to another recording of that type of music, or of that composer or performer.

Medieval music

(pages 4 and 5)

Instruments of the Middle Ages and the Renaissance, Vol. 1 (EMI)

Religious music: *A Dictionary of Medieval Music, Vol. 1, Monks and Troubadours* (Harmonia Mundi)

Hildegard of Bingen: *Canticles of Ecstasy, Symphonia armonie celestium revelationum* (HM/BMG)

Léonin and Pérotin: *Organa* (Lyrichord)

Minstrels: *Music of the Minstrels* (Telefunken)

Troubadours and trouvères: *Music of the Trouvères and the Troubadours* (Arion)

The 'new art': *Machaut, Messe de Nostre Dame*

Renaissance music

(pages 6 and 7)

Music at the Court of Burgundy (EMI)

Lute music: John Dowland, *Lachrimae* (RCA);

Madrigals: Andrea Gabrieli, *Ave Regina*

Church music: Palestrina, *Missa Papae Marcelli*; Tallis, *Spem in alium*

Baroque music

(pages 8 and 9)

Organ music: J.S. Bach, *Toccata and Fugue in D minor*

Flute music: Quantz, *Sei sonate a flauto traversiere solo, op.1*

Concerto grosso: Vivaldi, *The Four Seasons*; Bach, *Brandenburg concertos*

Oratorio: Handel, *Messiah*

Violin music: Corelli, *Violin sonata, op. 5, no. 12, 'La folia'*

Suites: Rameau, *Pièces de clavecin*

Classical music

(pages 10 and 11)

String Quartet: Haydn, *String quartet, op.33, no.2 in E flat, 'The Joke'*

Concerto: Mozart, *Piano concerto, no. 21 in C, K467*

Sonata: Beethoven, *Piano sonata, op.27, no.2, 'Moonlight'*; Mozart, *Piano sonata in A, K331*

Symphony: Beethoven, *Symphony no.6, 'Pastoral'*

The orchestra

(pages 12 and 13)

Mozart, *Symphony no. 40 in G minor*; Tchaikovsky, *1812 Overture*; Holst, *The Planets*; Prokofiev, *Peter and the Wolf*; Bartók, *Concerto for orchestra*; Britten, *The Young Person's Guide to the Orchestra*

Romantic music

(pages 14 and 15)

Waltz: Johann Strauss II, *The Blue Danube*

Eastern Europe: Borodin, *Polovtsian dances from Prince Igor*

Symphonic poem: Liszt, *Hamlet*

Schubert songs: *Erlkönig (The Erl King), Die Forelle (The Trout)*

Symphony: Mahler, *Symphony no. 8, 'Symphony of a Thousand'*

Opera

(pages 16 and 17)

Early opera: Monteverdi, *Orfeo*; Lully, *Alceste*

Opera seria: Handel, *Rinaldo*

Comic opera: Mozart, *Die Zauberflöte (The Magic Flute)*

19th century opera: Puccini, *Turandot*

Grand opera: Rossini, *Guillaume Tell*

Operetta: Johann Strauss II, *Die Fledermaus*

20th century opera: Stravinsky, *Mavra*; Luigi Nono, *Intolleranza*; Harrison Birtwhistle, *The Mask of Orpheus*

Music and Dance

(pages 18 and 19)

Dances of the Middle Ages and the Renaissance (Arion)

Dancing at court: J.S. Bach, *Minuet in G from Clavierbüchlein BVW Anh. 113*

Irish dance music: Altan, *Island Angel* (Green Linnet records)

Ballet: Lully, *Le Bourgeois gentilhomme* (a type of opera which includes ballet); Tchaikovsky, *Swan Lake*, *The Sleeping Beauty*

Dancing for fun: Chubby Checker, *The Twist*

Blues
(page 20)

Origins of the blues: *The Roots of the Blues* (Columbia, Roots N' Blues)

Early blues: W.C. Handy's *Memphis Blues Band* (Memphis Archives)

Country blues: Blind Blake, *Ragtime Guitar's Foremost Fingerpicker* (Yazoo)

City blues: Leroy Carr, *Complete Recorded Works In Chronological Order*, Vol. 1 (Document); B.B. King, *Live at the Regal* (MCA); Son House, *Son House and the Great Delta Blues Singers* (Document); John Lee Hooker, *Blues Brothers* (Ace)

Jazz
(page 21)

Early jazz: King Oliver's Jazz Band, *Canal Street Blues*

Swing bands: Duke Ellington, *Mood Indigo*; Count Basie, *Jumpin' At The Woodside*

Modern jazz: Dizzie Gillespie, *Big 4*

Jazz influence: Aaron Copland, *Concerto for piano and orchestra*; Debussy, 'Golliwog's cakewalk' from *Children's Corner*

Music in the 20th century
(pages 22 and 23)

Stravinsky, *The Rite of Spring*

Electronic music: Stockhausen, *Gesang der Jünglinge*

Aleatory music: John Cage, *Concert for piano and orchestra*

Computer music: Pierre Boulez, *Répons*

New sounds: Olivier Messiaen, *Catalogue d'oiseaux*; Varèse, *Ionisation*

Popular music
(pages 24 and 25)

Cole Porter, *Cole Porter Sings Cole Porter*

Rock and roll: *The King of Rock'n'roll, the Complete 50s Masters*; *From Nashville to Memphis, the Essential 60s Masters Vol. 1*; Elvis Presley, *Essential Elvis Presley*; The Beatles, *A Hard Day's Night*

Rock and pop music: The Rolling Stones, *Aftermath*; Fleetwood Mac, *Rumours*; The Eagles, *Hotel California*; Bob Dylan, *Blood on the Tracks*; Michael Jackson, *Thriller*; Madonna, *Immaculate Collection*; Prince, *Purple Rain*; U2, *The Joshua Tree*

Rap: Run DMC, *Raising Hell*

Reggae: Bob Marley and the Wailers, *Songs of Freedom*

Heavy metal: Metallica, *And Justice for All*

Punk: The Ramones, *Too Tough to Die*

Popular music today: Nirvana, *Nevermind*; Pearl Jam, *Vs.*; Soundgarden, *Superunknown*

Hip-hop: Public Enemy, *Apocalypse 91... The Enemy Strikes Back*

Musicals: Rogers and Hammerstein II, songs from *Oklahoma* and *Oliver*; Andrew Lloyd Webber, songs from *Cats*

Music in the Middle East
(page 26)

Hava Nagila, Israeli Folk songs and dances (Arc Music); Iran, *Les Maitres de la Musique Traditionnelle*, Vol. 3 (Paris, Ocora Radio France); Jaffar Hussain Khan, *Songs of Popular Islam* (Tokyo, King Records)

Music in Africa
(page 27)

Tabara, *Gambian Kora Music* (Music of the World); Adzido, *Akwaaba, Songs and Dances from Black Africa* (Arc Music); *The Drummers of Burundi, Live at Real World* (Real World)

Music in the Far East
(pages 28 and 29)

India: Gurdev Singh, *Keda Virtuoso Series*, Vols. 4 and 5 (Keda Records)

Japan: *Japon, Kabuki and Juita-Mai Music* (Ethnic Saga); Japan, *Splendour of the Koto* (Playa Sound, Sunset-France)

China: Shanghai National Music Orchestra, *Music of China* (Voyager)

Indonesia: *Bali, Java, Traditional Music* (Playa Sound)

Index

Acknowledgements

The publishers are grateful to the following for the use of photographic material:
B. Sokoloff/Camera Press London (page 7); Photo AKG London/Munich, Deutsches Theatermuseum (page 10); Clive Barda/Performing Arts Library (page 12; page 22, top; page 23, bottom); Catherine Ashmore (page 17); Aquarius (page 19); Tim Hall/Redferns (page 20); Peter Newark's American Pictures (page 21, top left); David Redfern/Redferns (page 21, top right); Fritz Curzon/Performing Arts Library (page 22, top right); Explorer/Robert Harding Picture Library (page 23, top); Retna Pictures © Photofest (page 24, top); Michael le Poer Trench/Rex Features (page 24, bottom); Dezo Hoffmann/Rex Features (page 25, top); Frank Forcino/London Features (page 25, bottom).

Concert for piano and orchestra by John Cage (page 23): © 1960 by Henmar Press Inc., New York. Reproduced on behalf of the publishers by permission of Peters Edition Ltd., London; Duke Ellington and his famous orchestra, *Cotton Tail - Fox Trot* (page 21): Reproduced on behalf of the Publishers by permission of EMI Records; Duke Ellington and his famous orchestra, *Boy Meets Horn* (page 21): Reproduced on behalf of the Publishers by permission of Polygram International Ltd., London; Count Basie and his orchestra, *Time Out* (page 21): Reproduced on behalf of the Publishers by permission of MCA Records.

The publishers would like to thank the following for supplying the instruments on the cover:
The South Bank Gamelan Programme, London (gamelan drum); Christopher Monk Instruments, London (serpent); Andy's Guitar Workshop, London (electric guitar); Bridgewood and Neitzert, London (violin); Bill Lewington Musical Instruments, London (trumpet and saxophone); Ray Man, London (wooden flute and lute).